# SOLO PLUS

# Alto Saxophone

## *with piano accompaniment*

## My First Recital

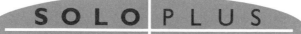

# Alto Saxophone

## with piano accompaniment

An outstanding collection of twenty-three light classics and folk songs
from around the world expertly arranged for the first-time recitalist.
With piano accompaniment in printed *and* digitally recorded formats.

Cover photography by Randall Wallace
Arranged and performed by David Pearl

This book Copyright © 1999 by Amsco Publications,
A Division of Music Sales Corporation, New York

Order No. AM 947452
US International Standard Book Number: 0.8256.1682.4
UK International Standard Book Number: 0.7119.6953.1

Exclusive Distributors:
**Music Sales Corporation**
257 Park Avenue South, New York, NY 10010 USA
**Music Sales Limited**
8/9 Frith Street, London W1V 5TZ England
**Music Sales Pty. Limited**
120 Rothschild Street, Rosebery, Sydney, NSW 2018, Australia

Printed in the United States of America by
Vicks Lithograph and Printing Corporation

**Amsco Publications**
*New York/London/Sydney*

# Contents

# A Frangesa

Costa

**Tempo di marcia** ♩ = 96

# A Media Luz

E. Donato

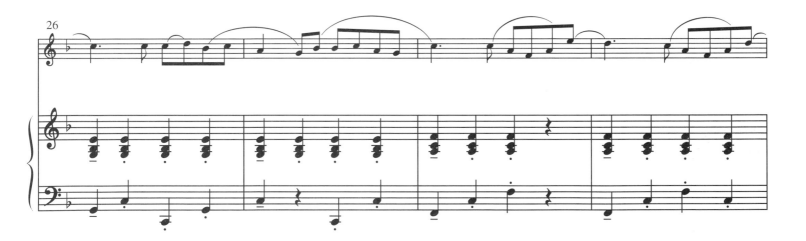

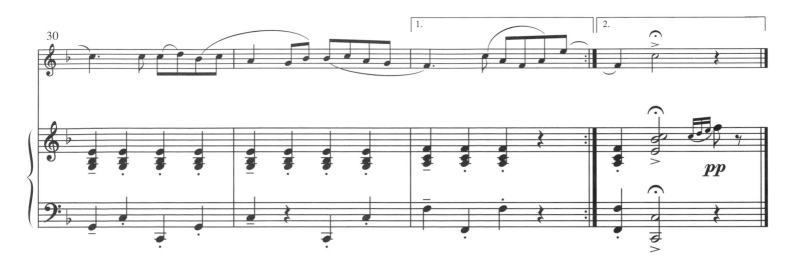

# Allemande

Franz Joseph Haydn

**Moderato** ♩ = 120

# Amaryllis

H. Ghys

**Allegro moderato** ♩ = 96

# Arirang

Korean Folk Song

# The Beautiful Jasmine

Ancient Chinese Melody

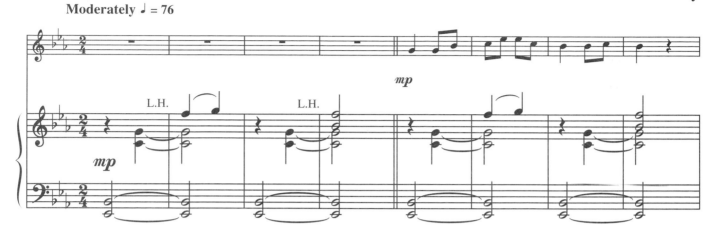

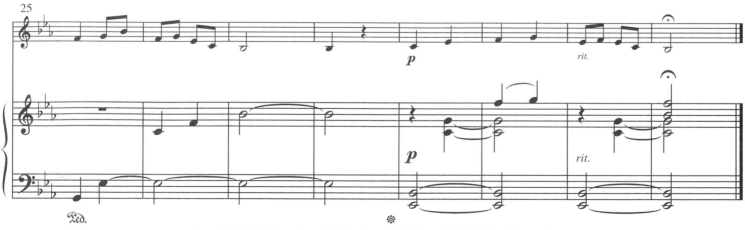

# Bourée

Leopold Mozart

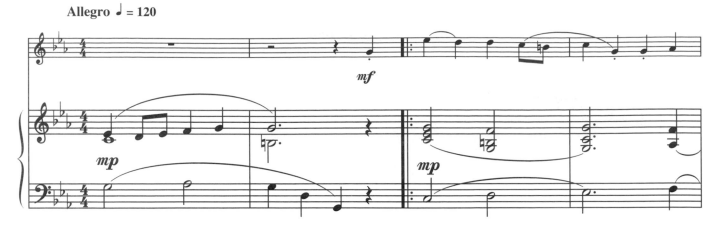

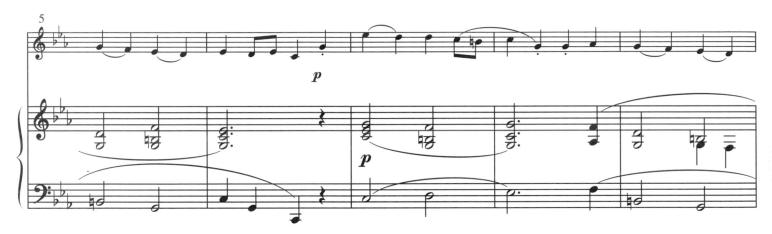

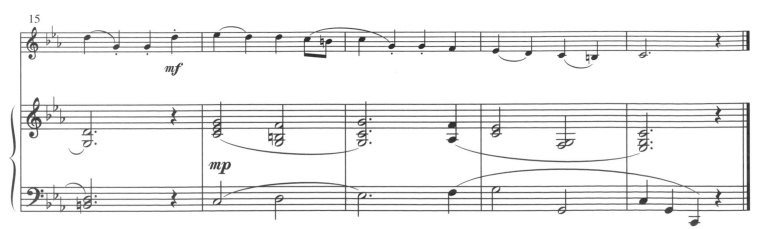

# El Coqui

Puerto Rican Folk Song

# Dubula
*Shoot*

African Folk Song

**Moderately fast** ♩ = 132

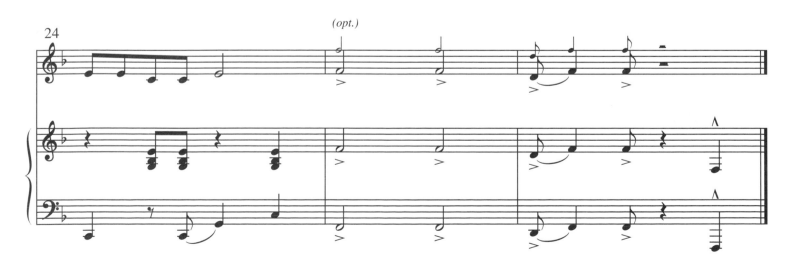

# Grand March

## from *Aida*

Giuseppe Verdi

**Allegro maestoso** ♩= 96

# The Cowherd's Song

Edvard Grieg